Loglines

A WORKBOOK OF STORY IDEAS FOR WRITERS

CARLOS PEREZ

AuthorHouse™
1663 Liberty Drive
Bloomington, IN 47403
www.authorhouse.com
Phone: 1 (800) 839-8640

Published by AuthorHouse 03/28/2017

ISBN: 978-1-5246-7540-0 (sc)
ISBN: 978-1-5246-7539-4 (e)

Carlos Perez has been published in:

Potpourri
Midwest Medical Ethics
Prism
Indie Reader
Pitch Weekly
Imagine This!
Penny
Masterplots
Theatre Training News
KC Stage Magazine
Perspectives
Number One
The Ecphorizer

Published Books by Carlos Perez

Tales from a Disturbed Mind
24 Tales to Pass the Time
Playland: For Adult Games
School Days: Tales of Teens at Weeping Willow High

Published Stage Plays by Carlos Perez

Folktales For Fun—Pioneer Drama Service
Caught Between Two Worlds—Dramatic Publishing

Produced Original Stage Plays

Cleansing Acts—Labute New Theatre Festival
In Hyding—Monster Box Theatre
The Other Side—Independence City Theatre

Produced Original Screenplay

Jeremy's World

Produced Screenplays as a writer-for-hire

Don't Look in the Cellar
Vamps in the City
666 The Ritual aka *The Occultist*
Monster: The Prehistoric Project
Agent Beetle
Metal Man
The Black Knight—Returns
Starquest: The Odyssey

Contents

Introduction

After over 20 years of teaching, 13 of which were as a tenured college professor, there is still one phrase I hear repeatedly from my students, "I don't know what to write about." There are quite a few places where one can find ideas—from news articles, from the media, from friends, from personal experiences, and of course, from one's imagination. It's been said there are a limited number of plots but an endless way of utilizing them, and I guess that's where the process of writing comes into play. Some of the enjoyment of creating an idea, that will be engaging and fun to write, is how to take a plot that has been used before and spin it into something new and exciting.

Contained within this book are 25 loglines and/or story ideas and five writing exercises to help you in your quest to create and get a story down on paper. The final page in this workbook is a writer evaluation sheet used to help a writer, or someone reading a writer's work, to evaluate what they've written or read. It's always important to get feedback, even if it's self-feedback, and hopefully, this important feedback will help you, the writer, to improve your work.

Consider the entries in this workbook as just jumping off points for your writing. The book has been set up with loglines, which, for those of you unfamiliar with screenwriting, are one sentence descriptions of your story. Generally, a logline names the protagonist and what the protagonist wants or wishes to achieve. An example might be along the lines of the following as a possible logline for *The Wizard of Oz*.

A Kansas tornado carries a spirited farm girl to a fantastic land of talking scarecrows and evil witches and the only way for her to return home is to fulfill a dangerous mission assigned to her by a frightening wizard known only as the great and powerful Oz.

Loglines are often employed to gain the attention of producers as teasers to get them to either read the synopsis, or treatment, or hopefully, the full script. The loglines in this book are designed to be teasers for your own writing and to get you started in the writing process. A blank pages is provided with each logline to allow you to expand upon the idea or use it as a spring board for your own concept. After that section is an extended version of these loglines, to give you an idea of how they might be extended upon. Once again, they're only a guide into the process of writing. Ideas themselves are not copyrightable items, but just thoughts on how one might create a completed story; it's a completed story, like a full script, that can be copyrighted, not the idea.

I've been a writer for over 20 years and the last eight of them has been as a writer-for-hire in which I've been writing as a freelancer for various independent movie producers and publishers. During this time, I've been asked not only to write full scripts of anywhere from 90 to 120 pages, but also to write ad copy, synopses of scripts, as well as treatments for scripts. For your information, a logline, as previously stated is a summation of the idea of the script in a sentence or two. A synopsis can generally be anywhere from one to three pages, while a treatment is much longer, going anywhere from eight pages and up. As to the amount of work I've written, it would include 14 scripts as a writer-for-hire with eight of those being produced into actual films, and an original produced screenplay, along with five full-length original screenplays, at least ten or more short screenplays, various full length and short stage plays, two of which have been published, and quite a collection of published poems and short stories, along with several published magazine articles, and book and stage play reviews. My writing background is quite varied and to be honest, writing is what I prefer to do, with an occasional run at acting and directing, and of course, adjunct college teaching.

Hopefully, you'll find this book helpful and fun. It's meant to be used as a writing tool for the independent solo writer, a workbook for a creative writing class, or a discussion writing tool for writing groups working together to help each other to perfect their craft. Remember that the idea is just the beginning of the writing process, the real work comes when you write and complete your story, article, play, poem, or screenplay.

I've spoken with many producers and directors who've told me how they had plenty of would be screenwriters approach them, but few who would actually complete writing a full length screenplay. If you wish to be a writer you must be tenacious, and you must finish what you start.

On the following pages are the loglines for story ideas; these are just skeletons, it's up to you to give them flesh and blood. Along with the loglines are more fleshed out ideas that helped in their creation. I'm also including a few writing exercises I use with my students to help get the creative juices flowing, and as mentioned, an evaluation sheet to help critique a written creative work. I hope you enjoy this workbook, and may your muse be with you.

Carlos Perez, M.A.

Writing Exercise #1

Take a look at a few of your favorite books, movies, short stories, or whatever, and see if you can summarize them in one sentence. An example previously given was for *The Wizard of Oz*, and went as follows:

A Kansas tornado carries a spirited farm girl to a fantastic land of talking scarecrows and evil witches and the only way for her to return home is to fulfill a dangerous mission assigned to her by a frightening wizard known only as the great and powerful Oz.

Now choose a few of your favorite books or movies and figure out just how you would summarize them in one sentence. An example of a logline I read for the movie *Outland*, which starred Sean Connery; was described in brief as "High Noon in Space," and if you've seen *High Noon*, you'll know exactly what the description means and how it applies to the movie *Outland*. Do this exercise with your own work as well. This exercise is good for allowing you to better understand and clearly state the core of your story. Many producers choose to read a screenplay based on a well written and enticing logline.

So go for it and give it a try. Use the following blank pages to experiment with writing your own loglines.

Loglines And Story Ideas

Logline

MY PROFESSOR IS A SADIST

A bright university student finds the diary of a renowned college professor documenting his sadistic psychological experiments on students and decides to expose him and even the score.

Now expand upon this premise in the space provided in any way you see fit for whatever medium/genre you like best. Remember, this could be a drama or a comedy or a combination of both. What would be the names of your characters? What is their situation? How would you carry out this idea? If you want to learn more about this premise, then continue on in the text to see how one might elaborate on the idea. Use the blank space to work out your treatment and have fun!

The Idea

A renowned university psychology instructor with an impeccable reputation notices three students (a woman and two men) who appear to be best of friends. He decides to conduct his own psychological experiment on them to see what it will take to destroy that relationship. He starts by favoring one male over another, as to weaken the friendship between the two men and possibly start a wedge between the three of them. He then starts making comments about how one male over another seems to be a good fit with the female, to create jealously between the two males. He continues this with hopes of breaking up the relationship, while taking notes of his experiment the entire time. A fellow psychology student who's been observing this follows the professor one day and finds the notes he's been taking and copies them and turns them over to the very students he's been experimenting on. It's now up the students to decide what to do next.

Is this what you envisioned by the logline? What was your idea and how did it compare? Discuss your idea with your peers, or if working solo, consider how yours is different from the one listed here.

Logline

DONATIONS OF AN ALIEN KIND

A prison physician notices prisoners returning to the same prison after recommitting crimes in a steady and predictable time table, and in his research he discovers the prisoners are part of an experiment being conducted by a covert agency within the NSA, and attempts to stop them anyway he can.

The Idea

A physician at a prison begins to suspect something is wrong when prisoners who volunteered for a military experiment and are released for good behavior end up back in prison only months later, once again as part of the military experiment. The aspect of them returning to crime is nothing new to the physician but the fact that they return in almost the same time frame and then re-enter the experiment is. He tries to find out more about these experiments but is told that it's part of a secret operation and to not get involved. He hires a private investigator to assist him in finding out what's happening to these prisoners on the outside, and together they uncover a diabolical arrangement between the military, the prison, and aliens from another world. Together they must come up with a plan to end these experiments.

Logline

A MISPERCEPTION OF LOVE

A child, who is prone to exaggeration, discovers another child imprisoned in a deserted house in the woods and tries to get someone to believe her before something bad happens.

The Idea

A young girl who is prone to exaggeration comes upon an abandoned house deep in the woods. She pulls a board off a window and finds that a child is chained to a support pole in the basement. She runs to tell the police and her parents, but since she's so prone to making up stories they don't believe her. She returns to the house to help free the child but the child won't leave for fear of getting in trouble by his caretaker. Plus, since this is the only life the child has had the child doesn't even realize anything is wrong with the situation. The child loves his captor. The girl continues to visit the child to keep him company and to try and find out just who it is that's keeping him prisoner. Eventually, she learns that it's the town mayor who is holding the child hostage. Now the girl must figure out a way to convince the town that the mayor they admire has imprisoned a child in a basement.

Logline

WELCOME TO MY NEIGHBORHOOD

An arrogant wealthy businessman must face off a couple of low life bad guys, living in the projects, who set him up for murder to test if he's brave enough to face them alone to get the proof that will exonerate him.

The Idea

A couple of low life bad guys out for kicks drug a rich businessman they meet at a bar and set him up for murder. When the businessman wakes up next to a corpse he must go on the run to find the bad guys who left a note as to where they can be found, a dangerous section of town known for its crime, drugs, and violence. Afraid the police will never believe his story, he must find them to clear his name before the police find him and arrest him.

Logline

WHO'S IN CHARGE HERE?

A newly elected third party president must get the proof he's discovered to the American public, that the power behind the U.S. government is indeed large multinational corporations overseeing the military industrial complex and using the media to control the hearts and minds of the people.

The Idea

A young governor has just been elected president. On his first day alone in the Oval Office an old man in an expensive suit enters the room. Fearing an assassination, the new president calls for security but they don't arrive. He tries to leave the room but finds it locked. The man in the suit tells the president to sit down and relax. The president does so, and this is where he learns the truth about being the president. The man pulls out a dossier of the new president's life, with all the good and the bad. He informs the new president that they have been keeping this dossier on him since when he first entered politics; including creating various embarrassing situations that, unfortunately, the newly elected president fell into and needed to be rescued from. The man explains that the president will continue to make appearances and speeches, but that the country will be run by a billionaire consortium. The president starts to balk at this saying he'll never cooperate and the man informs him that information will be leaked that will, at first, only be embarrassing but later much more damning. He is told to play ball or else. The man leaves and for a time the president plays ball but eventually can longer stomach doing so and starts to fight back and, of course, the leaks start then. Finally, he decides that he will tell all during his State of the Union Address, but the consortium is one step ahead of him and plans to have him impeached as being mentally unstable before he can do so.

Writing Exercise #2

Find a favorite author of yours and turn to an especially well written passage or section that really grabbed you and held your interest. Now, take out your computer or some paper, and copy these passages word for word. The idea is for you to get a sense of the pacing and writing style of your favorite author. By copying their work word for word you may get a better understanding of their style. This will not turn you into your favorite writer, but it just may give you some insight into their stylistic differences. I did this with one of favorite authors, William Faulkner, and I loved the experience. It felt almost like I was inside his mind composing the story with him. I did it in long hand because I enjoyed the tactile experience of writing by hand. However, do it in whatever way works best for you. See what you discover.

Loglines And Story Ideas

Logline

A SHAKESPEARIAN CHRISTMAS

In a spin-off treatment of *A Christmas Carol*, a mean-spirited Shakespearean actor or actress is visited by three of Shakespeare's characters in spirit form to get him or her to change his/her ways before it's too late. Realize that *A Christmas Carol* is in public domain, which is why there are so many versions of it out there, including *Scrooged* with Bill Murray, which is one of my favorites.

The Idea

In a spin-off treatment of *A Christmas Carol*, a Shakespearean actor or actress could be visited by three of Shakespeare's characters to sway him or her to change his/her ways. A possibility could be Puck as the ghost of Christmas past, Falstaff as the ghost of Christmas present, and Richard the Third as the ghost of Christmas future. If one goes with a female protagonist then it might work with Juliet as the ghost of Christmas past, Portia as the ghost of Christmas present and Lady Macbeth as the ghost of Christmas future. Any number of Shakespearian characters could be employed as we follow our protagonist's theatrical career.

Logline

WILL THE REAL MANNEQUIN PLEASE STAND UP

A woman is given an opportunity to turn into a mannequin, which is free to be alive only in the department store at night, to free her of the financial obligations and heartache of being human.

The Idea

For some reason a young woman has a fascination with a male mannequin. She doesn't understand why, but she's certain he is the splitting image of a past lover. One night she decides to stay late and hide out in the store so she can look at the mannequin more closely. Late after hours she sees the mannequins come alive. She quickly finds her mannequin is alive and is indeed her past lover. He tells her that he was tired of his life and found a way to become one of the store mannequins that come to life when humans aren't around. She sees that all of them are having a wonderful time without the daily grind of having to work to survive. Her lover offers to tell her the secret of how to escape being a human, that is, if she truly wants to.

Logline

IT'S ALL IN THE GENES

A scientist discovers why some people are instantly disliked by others and publishes his findings with a comically tragic outcome for himself and others like him.

The Idea

A scientist, who no one ever seems to like, is determined to find out why people have never seemed to like him. After studying the phenomenon for years, with other subjects like himself, he has found that there are minute genetics differences between normal people and those that seem to be rejected again and again. He determines this genetic anomaly is the reason some people appear to be automatically disliked. He publishes his findings and soon has quite a following of humans, rejected by the masses, looking for a cure.

Logline

NERDY BLOODSUCKERS

A group of nerds are set upon by a pair of sexy vampires and turned into the smartest, yet oddest, group of blood suckers ever conceived.

The Idea

An attractive female vampire and her female cohorts come upon a group of alpha male jocks harassing a group of nerds. She and her cohorts attack the jocks and drain them of their blood, and feeling sorry for the nerds, decide to turn them into vampires. Later the nerds wake up to the carnage and run away. In time, they all begin to turn into vampires with comedic, yet frightening consequences.

Logline

CLOTHING NOT SO OPTIONAL

A sexy couple of clothing designers set out to prove that it's what's not shown that makes you sexy when they infiltrate a clothing optional community to seduce its members by employing their sexy new clothing line to do it.

The Idea

In a clothing-optional community, a couple who design sexy clothing, infiltrate the community with the plan of seducing as many nudists as they can by dressing sexy, rather than going nude. They're determined to prove that a slight reveal of the human body is far more arousing than full nudity. If all goes well they'll be able to use this experiment to help promote their new clothing line as well as prove that clothes are indeed what make you sexy.

Writing Exercise #3

While out at your favorite coffee house or restaurant you might consider spying on those nearby. I don't mean literally trying to spy on them, but trying to get an idea of what others are like. Write down a description of them and listen in (not conspicuously) to what they're saying. How do they sound? What are their voices like? What are the cadences or pacing within their voices? Watch their hand gestures. Do they do anything that stands out or makes them more unique? I remember being at a fast food restaurant and a couple of men were sitting at a nearby table and one of them spoke in a rather loud voice, so it was pretty easy for me to listen in. And one of the things he did that caught my attention was how often he would say, "You know what I'm sayin'?" He said this quite often and seemed to be almost his catch phrase. Ever since then I've been waiting to use that with one of my characters. Don't forget to also describe the setting. How is the place decorated? What time of year is it? And so forth. This will help you in your use of description for your own work. Just be an observer for a while, discretely of course, and see just how good of a detective you can be.

Loglines And Story Ideas

Logline

I LOVE YOUR FEET

An adult men's magazine publisher accidentally lands in an alternate universe where it's illegal to reveal your feet in public, but okay not to wear anything else.

The Idea

A time traveler ends up in a new world where the inhabitants are all nude except for stockings and footwear. When he inquires why this is, he finds that the ankle and the foot are the erotic part of humans there and to reveal one's bare foot or ankle is illegal, unless one is married and alone within the home. In other words, the entire inhabitants have a foot fetish and must keep their feet covered when in public; whereas, the remainder of all clothing is totally unnecessary. He tries to explain the absurdity of this custom compared to where he lives and is arrested for fear of spreading his immoral ideas.

Logline

MAYBE THIS WASN'T SUCH A GOOD IDEA

To gain attention for his career, an actor makes himself up to look like an escaped convict; but once captured, rather than letting the actor go, the publicity seeking district attorney frames the actor to prove he's the escaped convict, rather than admit he made a mistake by foolishly allowing the capture to be televised nationwide.

The Idea

A young actor and his make-up specialist girlfriend decide to get him some publicity by having him pose as an escaped convict, whom the young actor resembles, and is currently being pursued by the police. Once captured the actor will remove the make-up and both will have demonstrated their prowess at acting and make-up. However, an ambitious district attorney doesn't plan to let them embarrass him and get away with it, so he prosecutes the actor as if he is the convict, even going so far as to falsify the actor's fingerprints. Meanwhile, the convict, figuring he's a free man assumes a new identity, and the girlfriend must now find a way to prove her look-a-like boyfriend isn't the man they say he is.

Logline

NAME THE TIME, BABY

A man dies and is sent to Heaven and allowed to go back to Earth as a baby to any time and location of his choosing and decides to go back to the past; however, something goes wrong and he retains his memories from when he was alive and ends up being born the first son of his grandfather whom he remembers from family stories died in a car accident on his tenth birthday.

The Idea

A man dies and goes to Heaven to find out that he can return to Earth as a baby in any place and any time he chooses. It seems that time is quite fluid and an individual my return to any time and any place they want. He decides to return to the past because he didn't care much for the present and is a little nervous of going back to an uncertain future. Usually all would go well with this process; however, instead of having his memories wiped out, he returns to the past with his present memories. Even as a child, he now has all the knowledge of the events of a man from the future who is now living in the past.

Logline

STOP ROSIE THE RIVETER

A misogynistic scientist returns to America's past to stop women from entering the work force during WWII, and the government sends two agents to stop him from succeeding to assure America doesn't lose the Second World War.

The Idea

A scientist, who hates women, has developed a time machine and is determined to stop women from entering the work force during WWII. From his perspective, this is when women stated working out of the home with real jobs and got a taste for it and never wanted to return to the kitchen. He plans on going back to stop that from happening by frightening the men in the past with the prospect of feminism and the death of the true American male. After he's left, the female president sends two of her agents, a man and a woman, to stop him, for without the women's effort during WWII, America would have surely lost the war.

Logline

LET ME SHAKE YOUR HAND

An alcoholic conspiracy kook tries to foil an assassin's plot to kill a political candidate, by protectively dusting his hands with cyanide then shaking the candidate's hand during an upcoming political rally, and then quietly slipping away back into the crowd.

The Idea

An assassin decides to go after a presidential candidate by protectively dusting his palm with cyanide then shaking the presidential candidate's hand to poison him and then escape in the crowd. Only one person can stop him and that's a conspiracy nut with a bad reputation for exaggeration and a history of alcoholism.

Writing Exercise #4

Have you ever felt there was more going on in a conversation than just chatting, and that perhaps someone had an agenda, goal, or reason for talking?

At different points in time, you, along with everyone else, are trying to achieve a goal. Perhaps you want to get a new car and you start a conversation with your parents that at the beginning of the conversation has nothing to do with getting a car. Over the period of the conversation you gradually manipulate the conversation toward driving, cars, or whatever in order to finally approach your goal of convincing your parents to purchase you a car.

If you watch movies, you'll see this often. The characters act and behave a certain way because they are trying to disguise what they're really after.

Take some time to look at ways in which people are talking to you or someone else with a goal in mind. Make note of a time in which they are doing or saying one thing when they really want something else.

What is the subtext or sub-goal of their conversation? What is it that they really want?

Write down a few specific examples of conversations in which you observed, or participated in, this form of subtext or sub-goal. What was said? What was it that was really going on? Did you do this yourself? What was the surface conversation about and what was it you were really talking about? What did you really want?

Loglines And Story Ideas

Logline

I THINK THIN, THEREFORE I AM

A mysterious shaman teaches Americans how to think themselves thin, but not how to stop the process once started, and now he's disappeared and a team from the CDC has been sent to find him to reverse the process before America starves itself to death while surrounded by food.

The Idea

A mysterious shaman from the East has perfected a way to think himself into becoming thin and has come to the United States to share the technique. Soon everyone is thinking themselves into actually being thin. The only problem is, they don't know how to stop thinking themselves thin; a minor item the shaman deliberately never explained how to do. Now people are dying of starvation while surrounded by food, and no one knows where to find the shaman to reverse the technique.

Logline
INTENDED CONSEQUENCES

An enemy government develops a deadly flu virus and gives the antidote to a select few of its population then infects the world, and it's up to a doctor and a secret agent to find the cure and expose the plan.

The Idea

An enemy government has created a new biological weapon. After having inoculated those in their populace whom they feel are needed, it unleashes the weapon onto the world. Soon this flu-like plague has spread across the globe, especially in America, where there are now riots and civil war. Soon the nuclear arsenal is threatened and the United Nations has authorized other countries to take over control of the United States arsenal to help keep the rest of the world safe. Only a biological researcher, his assistant, and a rogue secret agent can save the world from the brink of destruction.

Logline

A VAMPIRE BY ANY OTHER NAME

An entomologist/science teacher suspects a spider-human hybrid is draining the blood of people in a small town, but finds it difficult to prove to law enforcement, so he enlists the help of his high school science club to help prove it.

The Idea

In an Arizona desert town, many deaths have occurred with the cause of death being a large loss of blood. As usual, there are those who think a vampire may be responsible, but an entomologist has another idea, a spider is responsible and not just any spider, but one that can transform into a human at will. His job now is to prove it, find it, and kill it.

Logline

ALIENS FROM THE HOOD

Just before a transfer of a group of earthlings to a newly discovered alien planet and vice versa, members of a local gang slip into the facility and accidentally transport themselves to the planet, and sensing they've been tricked, the alien planet sends its own gang members to earth in exchange; however, once the mistake is discovered both planets send their agents to work together to capture and return the gang members back where they belong.

The Idea

Earth scientists have finally contacted beings from another planet, and Earth and this new planet have agreed to send representatives from their planets to each other. Not long before the date of transfer a group of gang members break into the earth facility and activate it and accidentally send themselves to the other planet. When the other planet receives them unexpectedly they determine that Earth has mispresented its best, and instead, send to Earth similar types of individuals from their own planet. Now each planet must adjust to the gang members sent to one another and the gang members must learn how to cope with living on another planet. Meanwhile, the scientists try to figure out how to rectify this mistake and get the Earth gang members back and send the other planet's gang members back home. Since both gangs have criminal records on their home planets, neither of them is any hurry to leave, and neither of the planet's scientists are in a hurry to admit to the mistake because the leaders of both worlds didn't like the idea to begin with.

Logline

CORPORATE ASSAULT SQUAD

A profiler and a detective must solve a series of assaults committed by a group of men hired by corporations to target high ranking employees they want to fire but can't without good reason, like poor work performance due to stress.

The Idea

A group of profilers/detectives have been called in on a series of assaults that don't seem to have any real connection. It seems those who have reported the assaults have been male or female and from different social and economic groups. One of the profilers/detectives gets a lead regarding what may be a team of thugs working together and decides to infiltrate the group. It is then that the profiler learns that these are paid thugs have been hired to assault high ranking employees that corporations no longer want on their payrolls, and who are being assaulted to affect their work performance and give the corporations a reason to fire them. The undercover profiler must infiltrate the group and learn just whose payroll they're on and how to bring down the entire organization.

Writing Exercise #5

Pick up a newspaper and start looking through the articles. All sorts of miniature dramas take place in the newspaper. I remember reading a brief story about a young man who had basically drowned in icy water and was brought back after 40 minutes of resuscitation. Apparently, it was thanks to the icy water that he was able to be revived. I went with this idea and came up with a short story that ended up being published in Midwest Medical Ethics. The story was fiction but did deal with the ethical dilemma of how long one should continue the resuscitation process before brain damage might occur, and in my story, I questioned what might happen to the soul at this point in time?

See what sort of dramas you can discover in your neighborhood newspaper and how you can use them as a spring board for your next story idea. Find an article and start writing.

Loglines And Story Ideas

Logline

I'M GONNA' BE ON TV

A philandering actor is conned by his wife, a TV anchor, into going on air with her and learns that she's armed with a bomb and a pistol and taken everyone in the TV studio hostage and now wants the viewing audience to vote, yes or no, for her to kill her philandering husband on air.

The Idea

A philandering actor gets a call from the police telling him that his wife has barricaded herself inside a television station and taken hostages. They have called him to see if he can talk some sense into her before they storm the place. Thinking this is a great way to get exposure the actor agrees. At first, he tries talking to his wife and she agrees that she will come out if he talks to her on air about their marriage. Figuring he can get even more exposure than any reality TV show, he agrees. He steps inside the studio and sits across from his wife with the cameras rolling and it's then when his wife reveals exactly why he's there. She announces to the television audience that she won't harm anyone there except her husband and only if the viewing audience votes for her to do so. In other words, his fate is in the hands of the viewing audience who is free to vote and call in. Taken aback, the actor tries to leave but the police won't let him, and the TV studio thinks this will send their ratings through the roof, so now the show must go on.

Logline

LOVE FROM A CAR

A man and woman, who are both married, start communicating with each other in separate cars during early morning traffic jams, and are conflicted about going further and meeting in person.

The Idea

A man and a woman in separate cars, who are often on their way to work at the same time in heavy traffic, start noticing each other and eventually start carrying on cell phone conversations and basically dating from their cars on their way to work. They talk about their lives, what they're wearing, and even flirt with one another. After a time, they both wonder if they should take it a step further and meet in person or if the relationship is better and more tantalizing as it is.

Logline

WORKER BEES UNITE

A geneticist has discovered a dormant gene that will allow genetically designed human worker bees to say no and not comply with the orders given by their wealthy owners, and plans to distribute a gas that will activate the gene in the entire worker bee population provided he isn't stopped by the corporate police.

The Idea

In the distant future corporations now run the world and the people live under domed cities due to the pollution outside. Thanks to genetic engineering, the workers have been genetically engineered to be passive and do only what they are told. Meanwhile, those in charge, who have not been genetically engineered to be workers, run the cities and keep everything working as they live in luxury. The workers, who have lived their lives like this for generations, know of no other life and have no desire for anything more. They work and they eat and they sleep and that is all. Since the corporations have fully obedient workers that can't revolt they can live in luxury, free of discontent from the workers as the workers take care of their every need. However, a geneticist who is tired of what he sees has been quietly altering the genetics of select humans to help create a rebellion. All the geneticist needs to do is release an interactive gas that will activate the dormant gene on the subjects he's altered. His plan is almost ready provided he can keep it secret from the corporate police and from his colleagues who already suspect he's up to something.

Logline

ARE TELEVISION WRITERS GODS?

A new game allows people to plug into their favorite TV programs and become a part of the show by becoming one of the minor characters; however, something goes wrong and a group of players are trapped and will die if their character on the program dies, so they must try to find a way to change the writer's storyline before the writer's storyline kills their characters.

The Idea

Thanks to new technology, people can now plug in directly with their favorite television programs. They aren't necessarily the leads but they are part of the show. The trouble is they aren't sure just what will happen to them since they replace minor characters within the storyline. For example, one might end up becoming an aide to the king, while another might end up beheaded. Everything works fine until there is a glitch in the system and those trapped inside the programs can't escape and must figure out how to get out alive when they've been ordered to be hung until dead, and their return device doesn't allow them to escape the fantasy television world they're entered. Will they die for real if hung or beheaded on their favorite TV program? Will their destiny be determined by them or by the writers?

Logline

THE JUKEBOX

A lonely bar owner buys an old juke box and, once turned on, it immediately starts playing tunes from his past that take him back to the actual events in his life when the songs were playing and gives him an opportunity to change his present by changing his past.

The Idea

A lonely man who owns a diner finds one day that the jukebox he has starts by itself and starts playing old songs from his youth that were playing on specific days in his life, some good some bad. He unplugs the jukebox but it continues playing. Soon he is taken back to these moments in his life and starts reliving them. After a time, he isn't sure if he's still in his diner, or in the places denoted by the songs. Soon he finds it difficult to locate just where he is in time and where the diner is anymore, or if it even still exists. There is a moment when he wishes the jukebox would freeze on a specific song and leave him in the place he was happiest, in a park with his wife and daughter, who died in a car accident years later.

Writing Critique Sheet

Title:

_____

_____

How long did it take before the story engaged your interest? Please give the approximate page number. What was it about the story that first engaged your interest?

What visual elements did the story offer that helped to put you into the scene of the story? Give examples.

What form of forward momentum was created in the story? How was this achieved? In what ways did the writer help in creating strong characters that you could visualize? Give examples.

In what ways did the story offer a beginning, middle, and end?

In what ways was the ending satisfying or not satisfying?

What more would you like to have seen in the story?

What do you think could have been removed from the story without harming the story itself?

What do you feel were the strengths of the story? The weaknesses?

What in this story really struck a cord or resonated with you?

Other comments:

Edwards Brothers Malloy
Ann Arbor MI. USA
July 13, 2017